A Life in Colourful Words

An Anthology of Poems by
ETHYL M. TEMPEST-MOGG

WARNBOROUGH
PUBLISHING

A Life in Colourful Words

All Rights Reserved

ISBN 978-0-9568667-0-7

First Published 2011

Warnborough Publishing
18 Lower Bridge Street
Canterbury, Kent CT1 2LG

publishing@warnborough.ac.uk
www.warnborough.ac.uk

To

Brenden • Daryl • Sheryl

Emma • Glenn • Louisa • Derek • Alicia • Gloria

Charlize • Riley

Warnborough House, Oxford 1973

Acknowledgements

Ethyl M. Tempest-Mogg enjoyed reading poetry as a form of relaxation, comfort and inspiration. She took pleasure in writing poems. These can now be shared with her family, her many friends and with all those who love poetry.

Thanks are due to Harriet Redman who typed the poems from the manuscripts. Gratitude is given to Bella Aklouf for her thoughtful suggestions and Anna Pollard for editing. Appreciation is extended to Julian Ng for suggesting a suitable title. Indebtedness is due to Daryl and Sheryl Tempest-Mogg who encouraged and inspired me to finish this long overdue task.

Brenden D. Tempest-Mogg

Contents

E. M. Tempest-Mogg.

Foreword

The poems by Ethyl M. Tempest-Mogg are timelessly contemporary, varied and thoughtful. Like all art forms poetry is about human expression. Herein, are poems that have been written to delight, to laugh at, to learn from, and to ponder. Many were presented at poetry readings and on Radio Oxford. Hopefully, some of these poems will become your favourites and meaningful as a companion, in times of joy and grief.

Readers of her poetry will be able to discern a positive and colourful outlook and, I am sure, be pervaded with the joy which Ethyl continues to impart through the provision of this fine anthology.

The Rev. Canon Dr. Richard G. Martin, SSC
Rector of Brisbane - All Saints'
Honorary Chaplain, Warnborough College
Vice-President, Warnborough Worldwide Alumni Association

Ethyl M. Tempest-Mogg
1912 -2000

Scion of the Scottish Earls of Kinnoull and Erroll, Ethyl M.
Tempest-Mogg was born in Glenelg, South Australia in 1912.
She attended St. Peter's Lady College in Adelaide, where she
was commended for her academic and swimming ability.
Thereafter, she studied at the Sydney Conservatorium
of Music and aspired to a career in opera. Her striking
appearance and powerful voice made her tutors believe
that she would follow in the footsteps of the great Australian
soprano, Nellie Melba. However, Ethyl's priorities changed
dramatically at the age of 19, when her mother became
terminally ill. Ethyl abandoned her studies and social life and
spent the next six years caring for her mother until her death.
Ethyl's first love had gone away to fight in the war and neither
she nor his family had heard from him. She presumed the
worst.

During his absence, Ethyl was pursued by the dashing Captain
Alan R. Mogg, an RAAF pilot who had acquired a pilot's
licence when he was only 16 years old. He had been trained
to fly by Charles Ulm, co-pilot with Sir Charles Kingsford
Smith, famous for making the first trans-pacific flight from
California to Sydney in 1928. At 18, Alan's father, a well-
known Sydney dentist, bought him a Curtis plane kit. The
Sydney Morning Herald in May 1936 featured Alan as a pupil
at Fort Street High School, building a high wing monoplane in
the back yard of his parents' home – "He hopes to fly it when
it is completed". And he did so for many years.

Ethyl was attracted to Alan's outgoing personality. He made her laugh with his constant teasing and pranks. Alan would often be seen tearing around Sydney streets on his motorbike, with Ethyl clinging onto the back. Ethyl's first flight was in a Tiger Moth piloted by Alan. When Alan looped-the-loop Ethyl, in her terror, pulled out the joystick and vowed never to fly with him again.

The couple married and after the war they moved to Manly, a fashionable holiday resort with the catchphrase 'Seven miles from Sydney and a thousand miles from care'. Her earlier admirer finally came home from the war and tracked her down, only to be devastated when she opened the door, obviously pregnant by Alan.

In Manly, Alan and Ethyl raised three children - Brenden, Daryl and Sheryl - and embarked upon a career in property development. Alan continued to indulge in his passion for flying. Alan acquired the famous Aeronca KS-162 owned by the Vanderbilt family of New York, which had been used for reconnaissance by the American explorer Lincoln Ellsworth, for his 1938-39 expedition to Antarctica. Alan carefully re-built the plane and often took his children for exciting flights.

Ethyl had loved travel ever since her childhood when her family used to move around Australia. This inspired Ethyl to be on the first tour to Japan, New Guinea and the Philippines after the Second World War. She saw Japanese civilians disfigured beyond recognition by radiation. In New Guinea she was disturbed by forest-dwellers being forced to dance naked for tourists. The devastation and misery she saw had a profound impact on her thinking, and she impressed upon her children the importance of showing respect for the lives, cultures, traditions and values of others.

In 1969, Ethyl, Brenden and Sheryl sailed from Sydney aboard RHMS Queen Frederica via the Panama Canal, to Southampton. They also took a grand tour of Europe – a motoring adventure of three months. The Tempest-Moggs were enchanted by England and especially Oxford. Brenden took the opportunity to study for post-graduate degrees at the University of Essex and later Hertford College, University of Oxford, which led to an appointment as a Visiting Lecturer (1971-1972) at Bethany College, West Virginia, USA. While in America, he was struck by the respect held for English higher educational establishments. Yet, many Americans believed studying at somewhere like Oxford University to be just an impossible dream.

It was Ethyl who initially envisaged an institution which could enable American students to study in the UK and have a taste of the Oxford lifestyle. In 1973, after a great deal of research and hard work, Warnborough House was founded in North Oxford. The opening ceremony took place at Rhodes House and Ethyl warmly welcomed the 200 guests. Among these were the Warden of Rhodes House, the Lord Mayor of Oxford, the Honorary President of Warnborough House Sir Christopher White, Bt., university and civic representatives, as well as many local and overseas dignitaries. Good-will messages were received from the American Ambassador, the Bishop of Oxford and Baroness Margaret Thatcher (then Minister of Education). The Rev. Dr. Karl Garrison Jr. spoke enthusiastically about the need for an independent college which would give American students an exciting opportunity to study in Oxford and experience its educational and cultural heritage. Dr. Garrison had helped to promote the Warnborough project in America, securing honorary sponsorships and setting up the first International Advisory Council for Warnborough.

Dr. Garrison provided many valuable contacts, including the President of the World Council of Churches; the Episcopal Bishops of the Dioceses of California, Western Massachusetts and South Carolina; the Chancellor of the Claremont Colleges; the Presidents of Bowdoin, Bradford and Hobart and William Smith Colleges; the Provost of the Catholic University of America; and the former President of Sarah Lawrence College. Dr William Chalker of the College of Idaho brought the first group of students. Warnborough students were given the opportunity to attend services at Hertford College Chapel, through the kind invitation of the Rev. Michael Chantry, who had supported the Warnborough College project from its inception and was to often visit Warnborough as a guest speaker. It was in this Chapel in 1987 that Ethyl's granddaughter, Gloria, was christened by the Rev. Richard G. Martin from Queensland, a personal friend of the Tempest-Mogg family and a key player in the development of the college. He was appointed Honorary Chaplain to Warnborough College by the Archbishop of Canterbury in 1986, an appointment he still holds, and he is also Vice-President of the Warnborough Worldwide Alumni Association.

Warnborough soon expanded and the urgent need arose for larger premises. In 1976, Ethyl organised the purchase of the Roman Catholic Plater College, situated on Boars Hill, a ten minute drive from the city centre. It had formerly served as the palace for the Anglican Bishop, Kenneth Escott Kirk (1886-1954).

In 1978, the adjoining property, 'Yatscombe' with swimming pool, tennis court, and woods was acquired as a home for the Tempest-Mogg family. In 1985, Ethyl donated it to the college as a dormitory for students and renamed it 'Yatscombe Hall'. The buildings and 13 acres of grounds underwent a sensitive restoration by Daryl Tempest-Mogg, a specialist in period design, for whom it was a labour of love. Students and locals were able to enjoy the tranquillity of its woods, secret gardens, lawns and rose-beds.

Ethyl loved landscape gardening and the grounds also incorporated a lake for ailing swans, and a large corral for abused ponies, delivered to her care by a kindly RSPCA inspector. Two ponies managed to escape into the garden next door and Ethyl was sued by a neighbour who claimed that the ponies had 'damaged' her croquet lawn. Ethyl defended herself in court against her neighbour's powerful legal team but sadly lost the case and had to pay extensive costs. Despite Ethyl's hectic schedule, she always found time for the animals. She knew each one by name and the vulnerable creatures would bask in her affection.

Yatscombe was the former home of Baron Shawcross, chief
prosecutor for the UK at the Nuremburg Trials. In 1919 it had
been the residence of Professor Gilbert Murray (1886-1957),
eminent classical scholar, a founder of Oxfam, the League of
Nations, and a President of the United Nations. It had become
known as the 'White House on Boars Hill' and had hosted
gatherings attended by Murray's illustrious friends, including
George Bernard Shaw, Bertrand Russell, Albert Einstein, H.
G. Wells, Aldous Huxley, G.K. Chesterton, Arnold Toynbee,
Mahatma Ghandi and Marie Curie. Boars Hill had long served
as a refuge for intellectuals and artists. Sir Arthur Evans, John
Masefield, Robert Bridges, Lillah McCarthy, Robert Graves all
found solace there, as did Matthew Arnold, who first wrote of
'dreaming spires', when gazing at Oxford from Boar's Hill.

Ethyl was an active member of The Boars Hill Association;
a community group dedicated to preserving an awareness
of this heritage. She would often bring overseas students
to meetings and introduce them to members such as Oscar
Nemon, the sculptor whose statue of Winston Churchill
is a landmark in Parliament Square, and Maude Rosenthal,
daughter of Oscar Levy. The Warnborough campus was often
used as a venue for The Boars Hill Association functions, for
fund-raising events for the Blind Society, and for SOFAAG
(The Society of Friends of Abuohia, Ashanti & Ghana), a
charity founded by the late Dr. Joseph Theodore Bradford
(Sub-Chief and Nkosuohene of Abuohia, Ashanti), Dr. Judith
Campbell (The Nkosuohemaa of Abuohia), and Sr. Dr. Petrona
SAC Schmitz. All three are alumni of Warnborough, and the
charity continues to provide health education workshops and
sanitation projects for people at the grassroots in Africa.

Ethyl's insight always guided Warnborough's development.
For the next twenty years Warnborough on the Hill became
a magnet for serious students, and provided them with
intellectual challenges which echoed the Oxford tradition.
Ethyl was an excellent listener and provided sound advice to
those who sought her counsel. Her popularity was due to
the personal attention which she gave to students and staff,
all of whom benefited from her 'open-door' policy, with many

women, in particular, turning up at her office in tears, then leaving much later in fits of giggles. Ethyl held a firm belief that people should be encouraged and supported, rather than blocked and criticised.

Her concern for student welfare was especially evident during the Iranian revolution of 1985. Warnborough's Iranian students found that their government grants had been stopped and that they could not contact their families. Negotiations proved impossible, so Ethyl announced that she was flying to Tehran, against Foreign Office advice, to "sort it out". The revolutionaries were amazed by the courage of this 73 year old, 4 foot, 11½ inch woman, and quickly submitted to her demands. When Ethyl returned safely with money and letters from the student's parents, she was hailed as a heroine on campus. The parents had not expected anybody from England to visit during that difficult time, let alone the founder of Warnborough herself!

Ethyl was profoundly religious and very active in the church; reading lessons and singing in the choir. She was a keen member of the Oxford New Testament Fellowship, which met regularly at Warnborough. However, she harboured a dislike for religious fanaticism. When her son Brenden was ten years old, she removed him from a church Sunday school where the children were being terrified by threats of hellfire and damnation. In her youth Ethyl had once organised a dance to raise money for the church. When she delivered the money to the minister, however, he threw it back at her and said it was "money from sin", which hurt her deeply. For Ethyl, true Christianity emphasised love rather than judgement.

One student from Ghana arrived with very few clothes, an old, near empty suitcase and a very anxious expression. Ethyl quickly got him fitted out with clothes and integrated into the student community. Today, he is a respected tribal leader, who has never forgotten this kindness and has maintained close ties to Warnborough. On another occasion, twenty students arrived from Namibia who had been tricked by a rogue agent. He had pretended that they had won UNESCO

scholarships to study at Warnborough, and they had sold
their only few possessions in order to pay him an exorbitant
arrangement fee, along with their air fares. UNESCO denied
any responsibility for them but Ethyl finally forced UNESCO
to agree to pay their living expenses for six months. Ethyl
also insisted that Warnborough, for its part, allow them six
months of free tuition and free extra-curricular activities.

Few however, dared mistake Ethyl's kindness for weakness.
Her son Daryl described her as "a strong character who
would take no nonsense". Despite her short stature, she
always insisted on wearing high heels which made her look
both commanding and elegant. Her formidable strength
came from her faith, her passionate commitment and her
sharp mind. She seized opportunities deftly as they arose
and always remained positive, whatever the crisis. One of
her memorable battles was with Oxford city council who
in 1974 had complained that Warnborough's huge intake of
American students would cause a water shortage in Oxford,
as Americans liked to shower several times a day! Ethyl also
championed various missions for justice and believed strongly
in human rights, women's rights and fought racism wherever
she found it. Brenden recalls "My mother had a huge sense of
social responsibility. She never said 'It's not my problem'.
If there was a crisis anywhere nearby, then it was her problem
too". Ethyl nurtured the long-standing friendships she made
in Oxford and around the world, and in turn, felt blessed by
her friends' support in all her endeavours.

Ethyl was never afraid of manual work and if a group of
students were arriving at short notice she would often clean
or decorate the rooms herself. Throughout her life, Ethyl
remained physically fit, she adored swimming, exercising
and ballroom dancing, especially the quickstep and waltz, an
interest that she passed onto her daughter Sheryl, who went
on to win many dancing competitions in Australia.

Throughout her life poetry had been a medium for Ethyl to
express both her private and public emotions. Many of her
poems were broadcast on Radio Oxford and inspired fan

mail from devoted listeners. As Ethyl grew older, she took on lighter duties but her business brain remained as sharp as ever. When it was clear that she was approaching the end of her life, her children fulfilled her dearest wish and took her back to Australia, where she enjoyed her last years at the beautiful seaside town of Cronulla. She was delighted to be near her daughter, Sheryl, who was a valuable comfort and companion.

Sadly, Ethyl never lived to see the college that she founded expand and move to its new headquarters in the cathedral and university city of Canterbury. She had always maintained the adage that "A college is not a collection of buildings but a community of scholars dedicated to learning". Nevertheless, it is certain that she would have adored Canterbury and found much there to remind her of her beloved Oxford: medieval buildings, punting on the river and a vibrant and creative student body. Ethyl talked repeatedly of a college that would "Cross boundaries and widen horizons". No phrase could better capture the spirit of Warnborough and it remains the college slogan to this day.

Ethyl's vision is immortalised in her poetry, and has a living monument in Warnborough College, which strives to preserve the fundamental principles that Ethyl lived by, such as respect for persons, pastoral care, hard work and looking people straight in the eye. Ethyl was a pioneer for opportunities in international education, and was endowed with a social conscience light-years ahead of her time. Today, her mission continues. Read on and enjoy her poetry.

❧

Old Age

I live in a house,
Quite all alone
With a heart that is heavy,
And frozen like stone.

Good days were many
In years gone by,
Now I am withered,
And blinded my eyes.

I sit by the fire
And I think, and I dream,
I wonder at times
What life really means.

Whether my many sorrows
Were only a test,
To point out to me
That God knew best.

❧

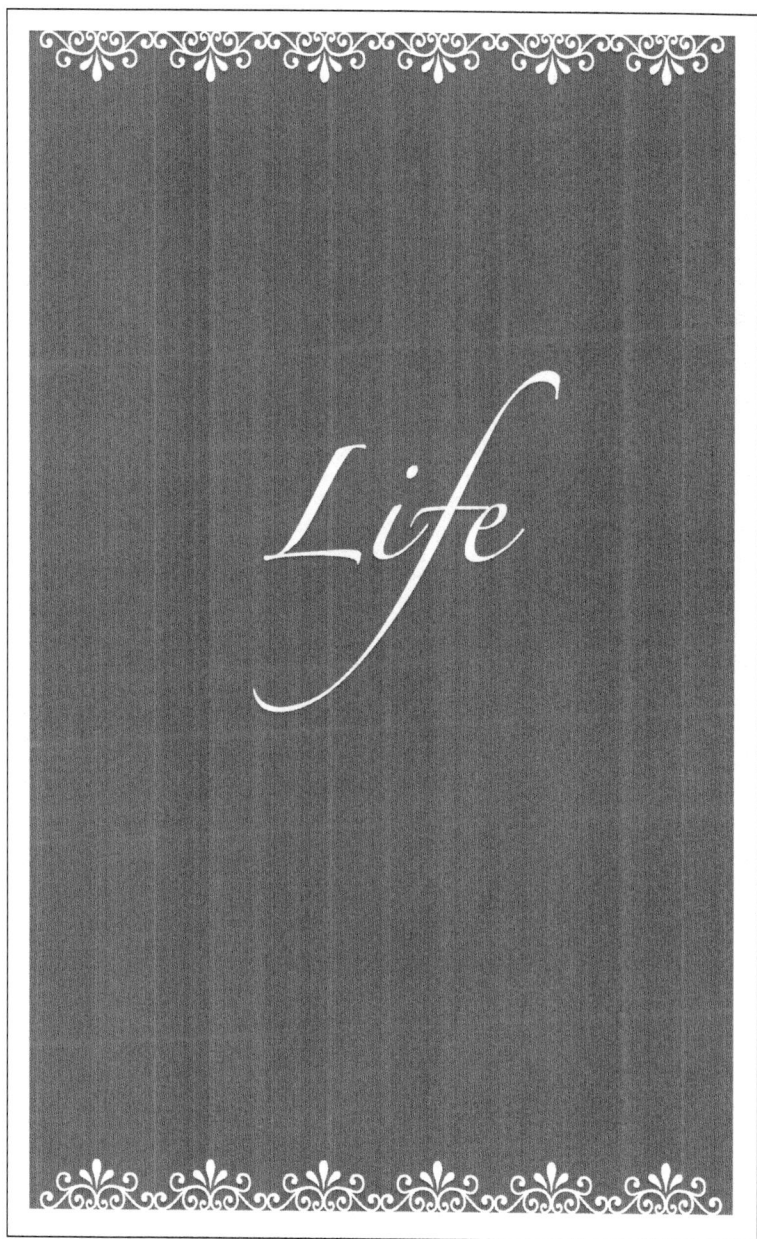

Life

Santa Claus

Once a year he came to our house
Dressed in white and red,
His beard was long,
His boots were black,
A woolly cap upon his head.
Just above his whiskers,
His cheeks had a rosy hue
His large blue eyes were shining
At the task he had to do,
To fill my little stocking
With just a toy or two.

I lay awake for hours
Until I heard a noise
Yes! Santa creeping in!
I closed my eyes so quickly,
Pretending to be asleep,
I knew it was very wrong
To lie awake and peep.

Through squinted eyes I watched him,
From my plate he took his supper,
Fresh jam, bread and butter.
Next he opened up his sack
And drew forth a doll for me,
He kissed it and blessed it
Then turned to me and said,

"This little doll will remind you
To never lie or cheat".
So don't pretend to be asleep
When Santa's on his feet!

A Wasted Life of a Hypothetical Genius

Drifting in the canoe of life,
Spent energy, procrastinating
Until the rapids caught him in a whirl,
Hurling him hither and thither
In a sea of wrath, the swift realisation
Of his nothingness, only idealistic dreams,
None achieved, and too late to begin.

The Wise Bachelor

Nothing this world owes to me
When I ponder and think,
Of the things I have done
And of things done to me.

I am grateful and glad
For small mercies I've had,
Like the fruit in the fields
And the birds in the trees.

The sun in the day,
The moon out at night.
All free for me,
And such a delight!

Neither influenced by others
Nor swayed by their charms,
I am just an old bachelor,
And do no one harm.

❧❦❧

The Major

The merry old major wore medals galore,
Won for courage in the Second World War.
At his club his friends all brayed
"Great chap the major, bedecked and arrayed".
He puffed and wheezed with such delight
To be distinguished in everyone's sight
Until he became bloated with pride
What would they do if he died?
For who at the club could replace his fame?
The major enhanced its worthy name,
Telling tales of war again and again.

Until one day a woman presented,
A youth whose birth had been resented.
Now everyone heard his angry son:
"Is this the one who left you Mum,
On that weary dreary night?"
The major stared in great dismay
His son had called his bluff,
What could he do, what could he say,
He'd surely had enough!
The son ripped the medals from the major's breast,
And pinned another on his chest:
A medal, not for bravery
But for what he should have done,
To care for a poor mother
And his own defenceless son.

❧❀❧

The Paper-boy

Running down the narrow street
With cheeks so rosy red,
The sad little paper boy
No time to lie in bed.

In the early hours of morning,
With the little ones asleep
His duty was demanding,
Get up and earn their keep.

Pennies meant so much
In those lean days of yore.
The thought of bellies empty
He had to work much more.

He wore thin clothes without a sigh
His feet were washed but bare.
His burly head held up high,
Boldly meeting ever stare.

"Paper, paper, lady,
Please buy one from me!
So we can all have supper,
Mum, the babes, and me."

Third Time Unlucky

Wet-eyed mourners stood by the grave
Around this hollowed spot,
He must have been a good man
To bring along this lot.

The wife stood there sobbing,
Tears ran down her face.
She knew she'd lost her husband,
A kindly man of grace.

It wasn't long thereafter,
She found another man.
Married him for companionship
And to work upon her land.

She worked this poor man night and day,
He felt so very ill.
She gave him the wrong tablet
A deadly arsenic pill.

Again she stood there sobbing,
The tears ran down her face.
She knew she'd lost the second one,
Another man of grace.

The third time she got married,
She didn't have much luck,
He was a lazy bounder,
For years they were stuck.

He made her do the hard work,
She had to do the lot.
He wouldn't even lend a hand,
She dropped dead on the spot.

It was his turn to mourn her,
As he stood beside her plot.
He wasn't even sobbing
Her money he would cop.

❧

An Epitaph to my Ex

Every day closer to the tomb
For you, and me, and even
The three from my womb.
Nothing to give,
Nothing to take.
A life of hell,
All a mistake.

❧

A Joke

"Laugh and the world laughs with you",
How often is this said!
But whenever I hear this proverb
It rocks me with dread.

I get up in the morning
Oh, so full of cheer!
Then I see the empty bottles,
Hubby is on the beer.

He has a violent temper,
Uncontrolled and vile,
Often gives me hidings
If I dare to smile.

But when I sit and look so sad
He always starts to grin
So perhaps this little ditty
Was invented just for 'him'.

I heard this world can be fun
But what's around the bend?
Only the pub which profits from
His drinking without end.

I try to understand the phrase,
"Laugh and the world laughs with you,
Weep and you weep alone"
I'm sure it can't be true.

If there is such a world
Where I may laugh and jest,
Would someone be kind enough
To send me the address!

❦

The Convict

I still love you dear,
Though you are locked away.
I know you love me too
Although you cannot say.

What made you alter so?
Tell me where I failed.
Why did you steal that money,
And end up in the jail?

Those handcuffs on your wrists
Are gripped around my soul.
The ten years that they gave you,
Will make you very old.

I'll still be there when you are freed
With arms outstretched you'll see,
Perhaps you will have learnt your lesson,
Please come back to me!

❦

*I*mpious Old Maid

You ask yourself the reason why,
Why you live and why you die,
Suffering little has been your trend,
Really nothing achieved in the end.

Single bliss has been your sin,
You have not sinned, you have no shame,
Your shrivelled mind believes this rot,
You've added nothing to this lot.

Scepticism you have condemned,
Sex you cannot apprehend.
Love you never felt nor gave,
Your life is spent and now decayed.

Perverted thoughts fill your mind,
Demoralising all mankind.
Your withered organs skulk within,
Dried-out in weathered skin.

Moss-grown thoughts green and hard,
Slump to nought in this façade.
Collapsed, deranged, a jumbled mess,
A life of hate and bitterness.

You ask yourself the reason why,
Why you live and why you die:
You've been no use to man or beast,
Impious soul, there's no release!

❧

*R*eflections

Have you ever looked back to when you were a boy
Or to the house where you were born?
Nostalgic memories are vivid in my mind...I recall
My room, my toys, and books...what a joy,
It's like yesterday when I was a young boy!
My first day at school, my heart broke, as the only
One I loved was parting from me.
She didn't know I had seen a tear-drop fall,
That made my first day at school a wrench!

The stolen fruit from neighbour's trees tasted better,
Better than it ever had before,
My first puppy, my first true friend,
I broke up when he died in the end.
To take his place, dad gave me a pony
To race.
I became a man that Fall and took a sweet girl
To my first school ball,
Heart rending sobs broke my heart when dad went away
To the war.
I comforted mum, like a real man
Undertook each chore,
Did all I could for her as before.
I graduated, that lifted the cloud from our house,
But it meant I'd have to reside in a college
No doubt.

Now it was worse in the home as never before,
I was at college and dad at the war.
Mum was one who had good faith in God
And the human race,
She coped well with dignity and grace.

Then the blood-shed war had ended, dad was returning home,
But his ship was scuttled and he was drowned,
A tragedy for her and me.
These wounds left a scar on her heart and mind, with the shock
mum went blind.
We sold our home and left the town, bought another
Near my college,
Where we could be together, and I could still gain knowledge.
After years it was over, I'd gained my degree rushed back to mum
So full of glee,
She'd had a stroke, I collapsed at her knee.
Tormented, I rushed for the doctor, the ambulance took
her away,
I prayed to God as she'd taught me, Oh God please let her stay.
She's had so many wounds, please, please don't take her away!
The stroke was light, my prayers had been answered
...she had back her sight!
My next step was marriage to one fair and true,
So good to my mother too.
Our babies were a comfort to her now, so old in her chair
...I still wanted her there...
For the years we have shared sadness, and love,
I love my mum next to God up above,
...A pure love...

❧

Tormented Past

Time had left its bitter scars,
Marred the beauty of her face.
Years of torment in the past,
Had wiped away her youthful grace.
The opened tomb claimed her at last,
Relaxed, reposed and still,
Laying upon the damp cold slab,
Death relieved her of her ills.
A bitter mouth and furrowed brow,
She carried to the grave.
Anchored in a material world,
A jungle of vice and greed,
Spiritual gains never unfurled,
She hadn't the time to heed.

Ye Olde Stocks

Their House

In trepidation they entered the house,
Which they'd bought for a song.
But once inside they were shocked
Everything seemed so wrong!
The walls were damp, the frames were green,
Everything rotted and not what it seemed.
Removing the lino, floor-boards half- decayed,
White-ants had feasted where it was laid.
They'd trusted the lawyer who told them to buy
They'd taken his word, didn't think he would lie,
Anyone could see it wasn't fit for these two!

But with their last penny spent, what could they do?
The land included a lake, but even this was a fake.
It was filled with rubbish and the fishes had all gone
Toxins and seepage had destroyed the land
Nothing could grow in this filthy sand.
The two ladies felt tired and broken within
The damp made them cough and reach for the gin.

Their kitchen was warmer but on the footpath,
Local lads would kick the door as they passed
The ladies regretted their purchase in haste:
Unbearable years of discomfort and waste.
Asylum staff claimed the first one to crack
The other one trembled in case they came back
And lonely, despairing and scared of rejection,
She took in a lodger just for protection.

Ada

In this permissive society it must give parents hell
To see their lovely daughter start to swell,
Ada was an academic; taught to have wide views,
She knew all the answers and especially what to do.

Encouraged to get on the pill, she took it for a while,
Delving in this sexy life, really made her smile,
Until one day a stalwart man, came into her life.

In his eyes she seemed quite pure, enough to be his wife.
He'd controlled his passions waiting for a bride,
Just for the satisfaction of a virgin by his side.

She played it very cagey when she knew that he was pure,
Didn't tell him of her past nor that she was pregnant too.
The wedding night was shocking as he lay upon the bed.
He thought they'd teach each other, but she taught him instead.

He became suspicious and he wondered how she knew
All the many little tricks, and some of them quite blue!

Her confessions made him shudder as she told her tales of fame,
His head hung on his shoulders in despair, and dread, and shame.
He vowed then to give her up, but the law was hard to break,
He knew he'd been taken in; his wife was just a fake!

❦

*F*ree from Inhibition

Her face began to alter
Her expression dull and dim.
A wild and sexy life
Made marriage very slim.

Boys knew she was an easy sort,
And there to have free fun.
No one asked to marry her,
Just used by everyone.

Until one day there came along
A man both fine and strong.
He thought she was a virgin,
So craved her for his wife.
He'd never had a girlfriend,
Never in his life!

While drinking in the pub one day
He heard the fellows laugh,
About his sexy Rachel,
Who was the local tart.

*O*ver-Sexed

I read a book by Patrick Boyle,
The funniest I've ever read!
Of a respectable bank manager
Whose lust was never dead!

He called into a pub one day,
The barmaid caught his eye.
He walked her to the hill-top,
Both heaved and moaned, and sighed.

Fornication with this shrew,
He had it night and day!
Until it made him very weak,
He should have run away.

More panting, thrusting, heaving,
She was heavy in his arms.
Yet he couldn't go without,
So enraptured by her charms!

One day a clot of blood
Formed in his right side,
He rushed off to the doctor.
Too late, collapsed and died!

❧❧❧

Honesty

For years they'd lived together,
With undercurrents strong.
He sensed he'd wed a cuckold,
And it was very wrong.

So if you wish to marry,
Your secrets you must tell,
Be sure and be quite honest
With whom you wish to dwell.

❧

Prevention

Cheer up mum, and cheer up dad,
Your daughter may be bad,
But don't blame your only daughter,
It's permissiveness you should alter!
What have you done to make it right?
To keep her perfect in your sight,
The pill was out when you were in
You had to marry to save your skin.
At least your daughter and her Bill,
Love each other through the pill!

❧

The Storm

I did not expect the storm to sweep
Your yacht onto that rugged reef;
The splitting of your wooden craft
And the heavy fall of your mast;
Nor to hear you call my name in vain:
A voice I shall never hear again.

Shipwreck

My house stood on the hilltop,
The wind was rushing by.
I heard a scream of people
And many children cry.

With coat and torch I ran towards
The frantic, desperate scene,
To see if I could help,
And what the cause had been.

The beacon from the lighthouse
Had fused so did not shine.
That's why this simple vessel
Did not see the rocks in time.

Then floating in the water
I saw someone's little daughter.
I jumped in and clutched her tight,
And swam ashore with all my might.

Perhaps I could have saved her
But the tiny child was dead.
The bashing of these mighty waves
Had split her hairless head.

*I*ntoxicated

Little ones called to mum
To come and hear their prayers.
But she had better things to do
Like flirting with the mayor.

One night while she was drinking,
She didn't hear their cries.
As they lent out the window
To see the cars go by.

Her little boy fell to the ground:
His tiny body - crushed.
In shock and in despair
Towards their mum they rushed.

She staggered to the window,
And poked out her hazy head
She fell into a drunken stupor
As she saw her son lay dead.

❦

The Seed was There

One consummation the seed was there
Thrust into the darkness of the womb,
Nurtured by the river of blood
There seemed to be much room.

As I lay snugly
In my liquid bed
Corpuscles passed by rapidly
Dressed in white and red.

For months I lay one side
Then wished to change position.
So I gave a mighty kick
Reminding mum of my condition.

Nine months I'd waited there
Till I could wait no more.
I felt I'd had enough,
So I pushed out through the door.

What did I get for my trouble?
But a smack on my behind.
I must say it was worth it,
I love this mum of mine!

Change of Emotion

Fourteen years he'd had the dog,
Who'd been his only friend.
This day they were to part,
With wounds he could not mend.

The tree was big, his axe was sharp,
He swung a mighty blow.
The branches from this lofty tree
Wounded his dog Joe.

The dog that lay there dying
With glazed eyes so blue,
His master sank beside him
There was nothing he could do.

The man's heart was heavy,
He knew he'd lost his friend.
He felt so sad and lonely,
And bitter without end.

Suddenly come into view
A women dressed in white.
He felt his pulses quicken,
She was a wondrous sight.

He thought she would be right,
To end his lonely life.
Although he had lost poor Joe,
He now had found a wife!

Jane

The clouds hung heavy in the sky,
The mist was falling fast,
The driver of this speedy car
Had a lurid past.

His driving was too reckless,
Everyone would say.
And he was drunk and heedless
On that fateful day.

It was Jane's fifth birthday,
We'd enjoyed a picnic out,
Then she ran into the open road
And did not hear me shout.

A car steered in a blinding rage:
The driver did not feel the bump.
Our little Jane's body crushed
Into a gory lump.

We screamed and waved for him to stop
He did not hear nor heed
Jane was crushed beneath the car;
And dragged along at speed.

That dreadful day we'll not forget,
Our piteous cries are often,
Crying for our little Jane,
Our baby in her coffin.

Years after we were walking
Along a country lane,
When we heard someone sobbing
As if in tortuous pain.

We peered behind a thorny bush,
And found a shivering boy
He'd fled from the children's home,
A place few could enjoy.

He ran to me with arms outstretched,
"Oh please don't take me back!"
Cried this skinny little boy,
With face so thin and black!

I held him tightly in my arms,
His hands clasped around my neck,
I knew I couldn't let him down
I held him one more sec.

My wife stood close beside me,
I sensed her trembling arm,
Could her empty life be filled
With this child's love and charm?

We sped up to the orphanage
To return the boy to care.
But could not leave when we saw
His look of sheer despair.

He sobbed "Please, take me with you,
I shan't be too much trouble!
No one loves me here
I'm just a tiny bubble!"

"I will never let you down.
I'll do everything you say,
Please give me a chance
Make this my lucky day!"

We huddled together and pledged
To love him come what may,
My wife was filled with hope
From that very day.

This skinny, desperate child
Could take our baby's place,
Give us a reason to live,
Through God's amazing grace!

We've never had regrets,
He grew to be a sturdy man.
We're the proudest parents ever
And we know Jane understands.

᠅᠅᠅

The Big House

I lived in a big house just across the way,
Then moved into a small one the other day.
The big one was a palace, a mansion!
The small one, the keeper's lodge,
What a difference it does make!

❧

The Land of Must

My thoughts wander to the Land of Must,
Wearied by existence, just
Tortuous melancholy – my lot,
Time spins needless turmoil on the dot.
No fantasy, my village furrowed with care,
It is all there,
Toll-worn hands tremble like leaves.

In the wind; my breath heaves
My heartbeat will rest before long,
No longer strong.
Limited vision; a dimmed view
Of splendid panoramic hues,
I am ready now to sleep beneath the dust
Wafting silently to the Land of Must.

❧

In the Sorcery of the Night

In the sorcery of the night
The wind mourned.
Eerie noises and wailings
Of those unknown, screamed
And pierced the air as if
Begging release from Hell.
I listened with baited breath,
My body clothed in sweat.

My heart throbbing in this
Cold, damp room.
Each ear-drum split, and
As my mind grew taut
I could stand no more.
My brain snapped – I screamed
Hurtling down until
I lay there alone,
All was hushed,
Gone.

When I awoke and peered
Around, I knew I was in Hell.
A screaming mob drew near
And the Devil spoke to me:
"You seem to have a weakness
For winds that howl, and rage
So join these evil souls
And scream, and mourn and wail!

I knew I'd lived on earth
In tension, and in strife,
God meant nothing to me then,
Didn't come into my life.
So when you hear the winds howl
And an extra mighty yell,
Remember,
It's the Godless ones
Calling you to Hell!

✤

The End

Weakened heart in an aged breast
Fatigues by endless beats,
Her withered body lay inert
On snow white sheets.

Silent relief spread over her face
Her eyes were dim and sad,
She looked towards the heavens
And thanked God for all she had.

✤

Reflections

True Heart

Look into your heart
The mirror of your soul,
Shocked at what you see
Commemoration of twisted thoughts.
Belonging to you, to them and to me,
Where only beauty should have been.
Cultivated weeds, pruned by your hand
Left no room for flowers to bloom.

❧

My Daughter

I miss you Sheryl, oh so much,
To have you near enough to touch
Is all I ask! And no more,
For in my heart I can explore
A depth of love for one adored.
I'm far away across the sea
But know you're coming back to me,
And when you come, the time will fly
But memories of a visit sweet
Will always be in my heart,
Memories I can forever keep.

❧

Mother

My love comes today to thank you
For the love you gave to me,
Memories of my childhood
Are filled with ecstasy.

My childish tears were wiped away
With gentle hands and care,
When I needed you for comfort
You were always there.

You guided me to manhood
And your seeds of wisdom grew
And blossomed in my happy heart,
All because of you!

My Dad

All the years I knew you, dad,
To me you were like a god,
But now you are icy cold dad
And lie beneath the sod.

Manhood

From baby to a man,
Try to do all you can.
For baby to man,
Is a very short span.

Many doors will open,
Choose the ones you need.
And give the world everything
That you may well achieve.

Patience, love and kindness
Can make your dreams come true.
So be a man of wisdom,
And God will bless you too.

❧

Cookies Cooked for Me

Not good-bye my dear
But just a fond farewell,
Not knowing you for long
Or knowing you so well.

The cookies you had cooked
Filled me with great lust,
The raisins, flour and currents
Oh, what a tasty crust!

❦

Dear Bengie

Why must you dig and cause this hurt
To rose-trees growing in the dirt?
They are there to bloom one day,
Don't destroy them to fade away!

Wee upon the grass so green
And leave the beauty of rose-trees!
Bengie dear, don't be mean,
Let my roses bloom for me!

❦

Realisation

I knew what it was to suffer
And to be without a friend,
Until I looked into my soul
And found much there to mend.

My soul was dark and gloomy,
I could see its bitter state
I knew why I was friendless,
With so much inward hate.

Deciding then to sweep it clean
To rid myself of fear,
To wash the windows of my mind
And see hate disappear.

I felt so very happy,
Light came pouring through
I had overcome my hatred,
And begun anew.

Many months it took me
Until one day in May:
My reward at last,
A friend who came to stay!

❧

The Reward is Adjustment

The culmination of episodic phases
From the cradle to middle life,
In adjustment and acceptance
Whenever there is strife.

Many bitter lessons we have learned
Since we denied the proffered hand,
That reaches out to save us
For He rules the sea and land.

But we are like human gargoyles
Silently content, in retrospect
All adversities to the novice we leave,
Intrepid circumspect.

❦

My Two Loyalties

There are two people I must please,
God and Brenden,
I must live with Brenden here,
With God hereafter.

❦

My Mother

Mother we loved you, Oh so much!
You met all of our needs,
Now you have left this happy land
To lie beneath the weeds.

❦

Feet

My stiff old feet are growing old,
They've carried me for years,
I took their strength for granted,
Now they bring me tears.

I bought my shoes too small,
My toes were bent and rough,
My joints were always swollen,
My feet were never tough.

I deserved what I had got,
And damaged what I've been given!
That is why I have these pains
And now I am bed-ridden.

So don't abuse your feet,
Buy shoes that fit your size
You are a special one
So choose and be more wise.

So Silently

Wearied courage and failing heart
Yet beat strong in tumultuous times,
But now fades, and wades into a
Tranquil stream,
Peacefully passing grass green moss
So silently ... so silently ...

❧

Tears

I cry each day
When the sun shines bright.
I weep each night
When the moon is white.

I have a love
That seems so right.
But why do I cry
Each day and night?

Alone I dream
When the stars are out.
Alone I pray
When I'm in doubt.

My haven of Heaven
Is a wall of tears.
My life is light
Without the tears.

But why do I cry
Each day and night?
Because
Peace has come.

When the world's gone black
Peace has gone.
When the clouds turned back
My tears have ended.

From haven to Heaven
Each day and night
My work is complete
Without much defeat.

The tears that were shed
Is an ocean of fear.
That's why I cry no more
For nearly a year.

❧

Oxford

"Oxford, the most prestigious academic city in the world is reputed to place in the history of man, a memory of immortality in a blaze of glory."

"Many students have come from all parts of the world to sit at the feet of learned men and return enriched by knowledge and culture, and sublime in strength and morals."

"The spirit of Oxford infects the humble and the meek, encourages the weak to take up the challenges fortified by historic ambitious Oxonians in a shrine of glory."

"Behind the portals of college doors, lies the knowledge of centuries fanned by the youth of today."

"Shoots spring from Oxford budding a field of wisdom, the fruits of whose labours yield."

*W*elcome

When you go back to the States,
And forgot what you have seen,
Pick up this little book,
And revive your fading dream.

Memories of old Oxford,
And the wisdom you have gleaned.
Relive those happy moments
At Oxford in your schemes.

These poems may stir memories
Of your stay, short yet sweet
With colleges and their students
In almost every street.

Of parks and gardens all in bloom,
With thriving churches too
Do come back and see us soon,
We'll always welcome you!

᪡᪥᪡

Arouse Ambition

If you are not an academic,
To Oxford you must come.
Ambition rises in your heart,
To fare like everyone.

Don't feel shy of scholars,
They've had to work like hell
To study for their degrees,
Which they deserve so well.

If a seed falls into your mind,
Nurture it with knowledge;
Watch it grow and bloom until
You enter an Oxford college!

❦

Oxford Fun

How can I tell the whole story,
Of Oxford in all its glory!
Of churches old, steeples high,
Of sub-fusc gowns, of scholars' sighs!

Curious shops in busy streets,
Scruffy jeans and sandaled feet.
Dark old clothes, yet happy faces,
We saw them there, in many places.

College libraries' books are stacked,
Students in theatres, fully packed.
Tourists overcrowd the streets,
Mouths agape, oh what a treat!

To see these people from countries far,
With faces shining like twinkling stars.
Car parks full, and in a queue,
Not a space for me or you.

The Open Market students rush,
To buy their veggies, a must!
Wobbly bikes whizz round the town
Knocking tourists to the ground.

The bull-dogs watch for scholars late,
Refusing entrance through college gates.
They know the rules, they close at ten,
God help these scholars if caught by them!

Romantic punting on the river
Where lovers swoon and shiver.
Shrill chirpings from the birds above,
Watching students fall in love.

Sweet strawberries in season,
With thick white clotted cream,
Served to students while plays
Are performed upon the greens.

Meadows wide where horses roam,
Children play on cobbled stones.
Tramps lie in pastures green,
Harmless ones so sad to see.

This is just a remembrance poem,
Of Oxford in summer hue
For there is much to tell,
And lots to see as well.

If you are a tourist,
It's just the place to come!
Let this city inspire you,
As it welcomes everyone.

❧

Sunny Day in Oxford

Have you been to Oxford,
On a sunny day?
Or seen her lovely gardens,
In the month of May?

It is a busy city,
Tourists come and go.
Students bright and witty,
Wafting to and fro.

The colleges seem gloomy,
Until you go inside,
And see the splendid gardens,
That are Oxford's pride.

This wondrous mass of colour,
Will chase your blues away.
If you care to come to Oxford
On a sunny day!

❧

Beginners' Class

We sat around a table
To give our point of view
Of someone else's novel,
A painful thing to do!

Ten hopefuls waited eagerly
To hear some words of praise,
But the critics' summing up
Left us in dismay!

Hers was vivid, his was strong
Some made no sense at all
And some were weak
Some just wrong.

We plodded on with weary hearts
Struggling with our pride
We were there to learn an art:
To see our work from outside.

Perhaps our cherished notes,
Like precious stones
Would help us gain more knowledge
From this Oxford college.

༄

An
Unforgettable Tutor

Memories of your friendship
Will forever shine,
Like a beacon on a dreary hill
For now and all of time.

In the morning you came in smiling
In a happy sort of way.
Your devotion to your students
Left you drained at close of day.

Tears were hidden in your heart
Yet a smile for everyone,
Your love for all the students
Dazzled like the sun.

Come back to us again one day
Share with us your knowledge,
Both staff and students miss you
At Warnborough College.

❧

*P*ast Students

Many thoughts were sweet and kind,
Of foreign footsteps left behind
On grass so green at Warnborough College,
Where they gained much knowledge.

We wish you happiness in all you do,
And to your own self be true.
Remember us in lonely hours
And Warnborough will think of you!

Examination Schools

In the High as you walk by,
You'll see the Examination Schools,
All exams are taken there,
It's the university rule.

Strung-up nerves and faces pale,
Clammy hands and collars hot
The atmosphere inside this door,
Is like a funeral plot!

The silence is over-powering,
As they creep their way inside.
They wish it were all over,
Exams they can't abide!

But these are courageous students,
They have a job to do.
When you see them looking scared
Just pray they all get through!

❧

Graduation Day

My study hours are over,
Graduation Day is here!
I feel most excited,
To hear the students cheer!

The Chancellor stood tall and proud,
He called me by my name,
My heart began to tremble,
My legs did just the same.

And as I walked the narrow aisle,
I did not see the step
Fell into his arms,
Held tight against his chest!

His broadened grin was good to see,
I was afraid - distraught
But he understood the students' nerves,
I knew when I was caught!

❧

Nature

Little Violet

Oh little violet, how sweetly you grew,
When we first met
I fell in love with you!
The fragrance of your tiny petals
Lingers still as you bloom.

I took you home and vased you there,
You stood the test of time.
Exuding your perfume rare,
For a while you were mine.

But had I left you there
To bloom upon the hill,
You would be alive today
With your friends, the daffodils.

Hot hands scorched your green stalk,
Wrenching you from field to house,
You ended up on my compost heap,
Yet your friends grew on the hill.
I'm sorry now I picked you there,
And took you from the daffodils.

⚜

Trees were Green

The trees were green
The lawns well-groomed,
The borders pristine
And buttercups bloomed.
Edges straight with bordered flowers,
Sprinkled gently by April showers.
Children played
Upon the green
Happy sight
To be seen!

❦

The Apple Tree

Bursting forth from branches keen,
Apple blossoms of pregnant spring,
Minute flowers, and leaves pale green,
Smiles to all, they always bring.

Weeks go by before they're ripe,
Kiddies wait in awe
To pick these ripened apples,
The simplest joy of all!

❦

Approach of Summer

Spirits stir at the approach of summer
Bestowing warm rays after days of gloom,
Upon those who suffer in damp cold rooms.
No profit is demanded by the sun,
It is shared with the small, the big and the tall,
With each and every one.

❦

Summer Before the Autumn

Summer fades before the autumn,
Withered shrubs rot and decay
Snuggling back into the earth,
Sowing seeds upon the way
For another summer's grand display.

❦

Disappointment

I felt happy in every way,
For this was the month of May.
Flowers in bloom, oodles of room,
To romp and flirt through June.

That burst of summer did not last,
The clouds hung low in the sky,
I felt my thoughts darken
As I watched the passers-by!

I forgot to take my rain coat,
With its hood to cover my head
Didn't think I'd need it,
Wore a summer's dress instead.

Then the rain was falling fast,
I was chilled right to the bone,
I wish I had not seen the sun
But read a book at home.

Artists' Delight

Heavy clouds of stubborn grey,
Hourly called in early May,
Blurred the moon and rising sun.
Artists moaned, their work undone,
Listening to the wind that grew.
With harsher puffs, as flagged
Atoms shuffled high enough,
To see the grey skies part and
Once more turned to blue.
Dear complete colour!
Then all at once upon the grange
Fairy land appeared.
Buttercups, tulips, daffodils and stocks,
Rosemary, lavender, forget-me-nots!
Shimmering colours turning loud
Against the searing blue,
Artists learned and snubbed the clouds
As sky rolled away.

❧❀❧

When You Whistle in My Tree

Little birdie, are you happy
When you whistle in my tree?
Though alone, I'm not lonely
For each morning you wake me.

When spring makes way for summer
And you chirp the whole day through,
I know this happiness cannot last
Neither for me, nor for you.

But the little bird had sense enough
To fly, far, far away.
Shunning dreary winter
With its dismal, dark, cold days.

She is called by the sun, her brother
To the lands where she may chirp,
Among the trees, to wake some other
Alone on nature's perch.

Alarm

It's needless to use my alarm,
Early birds do wake me
With their twittering charm,
Telling me it is early morn,
It's summer, and so warm.

Their chirping and trilling
Fills the air with celebration
I find it very thrilling,
And listen with elation.

Fluttering of wings, coo-ing of doves
Can be heard from high up above,
They wake me so early
I'm glad to get up,
Just to hear these birds
Is alarm enough!

❦

My Rose

Swaying in the breeze on stately stem,
Her perfume wafting through the air,
Hidden behind the garden wall,
Blooming so lovely there!

I stared at her so fondly,
I called her by her name.
Rose, Rose, don't die yet,
Do bloom for me again!

She could not hear,
Nor could she speak,
As each day passed,
She grew so weak…

Colour fading,
Perfume faint,
My lovely Rose,
Pure as a saint!

The Fairies

They feel the sun and see the moon
The Southern Cross that lights the way,
Pixies, gnomes, fairies and elves,
When all's asleep at the close of day,
That's when they come out to play!

Dancing through the dusky meadow
Red-gold caps of blue,
Nimble legs in tiny stockings
Mirrored in the sparkling dew.

Playing in the fields of clover,
Playing in the foliage green,
Playing on a flowered carpet
On a throne reposed their queen.

Prolonged frolics ceased at last,
Even fairies like to rest
The immortal creatures vanished
For they were but the flowers' guests.

༺❁༻

Snowflakes

White snowflakes fell from the sky.
The first time I ever saw them
Was a thrill and surprise.
The grounds and the lawns
Were changing in every way
Before they looked so forlorn
And winter seemed so grey.

I waited to see
What they would do,
As they fell from the sky
So crisp and new
Landing in layers
Delicate and free
Dancing around
An old chestnut tree.

The park was alive
With screams of delight
As children rushed out
In the brilliant white.

In less than a hour
They had gathered enough,
To make a snowman
From this white frozen fluff.

He had melted away
By the end of the day,
But memories of flakes will remain,
As this white snowy stuff
Makes me nostalgic enough,
To watch them again, and again!

❦

The Snake

Rustling under the autumn carpet
A louder noise was heard,
Mother snake was restless
To reach her hole reserved.

Then the snake found her place
And gently slid inside,
Covered by the autumn leaves
No one saw her hide.

❦

*T*he Moon in Orbit

Irritated by the approach of man
And robbed of divine privacy,
The moon showed displeasure
As astronauts bruised the surface.
Of her realm as uninvited guests,
Millions of years she was the idol of the stars
Remote and mysterious.

My moon, your moon, our moon
She casts a spell of romance for lovers,
Yet no room for stalking man to invade her parlours.
On and on she spins the same old route
Yet a different scene each time she passes by.

Peeping behind the clouds
To watch the world on high.
To the ends of the earth,
To the back of beyond
Her tortoise pace is never wrong.

As she spins, and spins, on and on
In the night, all day long,
The moody moon sulks in the winter
Because the sun takes a turn to see,
Just what the moon has been watching
On our land and mighty seas.

❧

Spider's Web

Woven threads in the old roof rafters
Mr. Spider delights in wicked laughter,
As he weaves away his work completed
To trap the flies who die defeated.

"Come into my tavern Mr. Fly
Drink of my juices, and stay a little while",
The greedy fly was tempted by his brew,
So into the bar the little fly flew.

The little fly drank deep and neat
When his legs began to falter,
The wicked spider laughed with glee
As he led him to his altar.

By then the drunken fly passed out
Into the spider's mouth,
Too late for him to fly away
Or give a mighty shout.

❧

Australia

*O*utback

Rays of the sun, the cold of the night,
I was lost in a forest of terror,
Forbidden to me this forest to see,
I knew that I was in error.

No water to drink, and scorched by the sun,
Torn by thorns, I could not succumb
Or run to the shade of the trees,
I lay inert, and dared not breathe
To relieve the agony in my soul,
As a snake crawled over me!

Bitten by ants, I began to scream
Arousing the birds high up in the trees,
Dingoes snarled behind tall grass,
No hope of them saving me!
A feast of flesh for vultures there
Stared waiting for my last breath,
A shot I heard, the bird it died.

Two strong arms then picked me up
And carried me to my home.
Only for this hunter
I should have died alone!

So listen to the warnings
Given by those you love,
Stay at home, and play with toys,
Beware the dangerous scrub!

❦

*G*olden Carpet

Beetles, insects, snakes and birds
Have ever so much fun.
Romping under flowers,
Bronzed by mother sun.

It doesn't last very long
This sun-kissed tent for lovers.
The wind in jealousy and spite
Blows away their cover.

The insects must wander back
To a dull and dismal life.
A grey hole or a burnt-out tree,
A cause for grief and strife.

They are sad these tiny insects,
They know it won't last long.
This lovely golden carpet,
On which they frolicked on.

Tiny insects play hide-and-seek
Beneath this golden spread,
Twittering birds could be heard,
"Where are they hid?" they said.

Sharpened beaks and alerted eyes
These insect lovers found
Frantic thrusts beneath each leaf,
Dragged them from the ground.

Rustling under the golden carpet,
Slid one predator alone.
Mother snake was restless
To reach her hidden home.

On the ground the autumn leaves
Had fallen from their mighty trees,
Brown and yellow, and of rust,
It was their turn to fall to dust.

❦

My Home Land

I came from a country far away,
Where it is sunny every day.
I miss the swimming, the surf and sand,
Tropical fruits fresh from the stand,
My friends were appalled that I'd leave them behind,
To come to England where the sun seldom shines!
Although it is nice to see your fields and trees,
The churches are cold as I pray on my knees.
But when winter has passed and the plants start to leaf,
The garden starts singing and softens my grief.

❦

Down Under
(I must go back!)

I want to go down under to the land where I belong,
Sunshine and the beaches, my need is very strong.
It's called the lonely continent by those who travel hate,
Yet everyone you meet soon becomes your mate.

Wild flowers abound, gum trees are thick and tall,
In wide open spaces, I hear the animals call.
Majestic mountains stand so high and proud,
Over which the sun hangs with nimbus clouds.

The sky is a mass of twinkling stars,
Guiding travellers from afar,
Lost in the realm of heat and fires
This is the land that I desire.

I want to sail to feel the salt-sea spray,
With sails flapping in a triumphant display.
I want peace as I fish from my little boat,
And jump into the water to swim and float.

Nostalgia stifles me while I am far away
I sit and pray in my cold damp room,
For I must go back where I belong,
Where I can flower and bloom!

❧

The Jackeroo

With horse and sodden saddle,
This dusty Jackeroo
Rode far and wide,
To find his kangaroo.

The country over-ridden
With kangaroos galore,
A huntsman shot a mother,
And many, many more.

In blazing sun the roo had lain,
Heavy with a little one,
Jackeroo found her there,
Dying in the sun.

He knelt beside her ruptured flank,
The wound was bleeding fast,
Probing with his pen-knife
Found the bullet at last.

She died within a moment,
He knew she would not see,
The baby she had carried
From whom she could not flee.

Desperately the Jackeroo,
Thought to save its life.
Squeezed and pushed the baby,
Then cut the cord so tight.

Shaking he took off his shirt,
To wrap the baby in,
This tiny little kangaroo,
He would take home with him.

First he dug a hole so deep
Then laid the mother inside.
Denying hungry buzzards
The food they had espied.

Jackeroo, Jackeroo,
What more could you do?
To help your friend the kangaroo,
When the little roo was due.

Harsh Land

Our land had grown sluggish deprived
Of the tears from heaven,
Winds raged in anger for want of trees
To unfurl, branches to uncurl,
The earth sulked and erosion swept away
Millions of particles of dust to a
New and happier world.
Undulating hillocks, one vast open grave
For cattle and sheep
Deprived of water, only salt-bush to eat,
No strength to leap to further fields
With grass so deep.
A grim and ghastly sight of barren
Land and wasted might.
In the far distant lull, the roar of the falls,
But none came our way, not one drop at all,
For it fed the lands to the other side
To the rich, not the poor,
Their fertile land and grass green wide,
They had it all.
Yet, steeled against inertia, near-spent fires
Fanned by renewed courage, this man
His strong-armed work, once more began.

❧

Hard Times in the Outback

Our house was a crooked house
Slanting further through the years,
Swayed by the rhythm of the winds,
The rafters creaked with tears.

The floor-boards on the veranda
Swelled by the heat of the sun,
We gathered in the evenings
To pray for rain to come.

The roof leaked, the chimney smoked,
Yet the hearth was neat and clean.
One pair of hands did all the work,
My mother made it gleam.

No flowers grew in the garden,
No dampness in the old worn boards.
White-ants came to inspect us
Then marched away in hordes.

The kitchen was large and airy,
Four chairs, and a crooked table,
The old stove we kept on feeding
With coal from our shabby stable.

Our lounge room sofa had a hump
Just like a camel's back,
For many years we jumped on it
To feel the springs spring back!

The rocking chair stood near the fire
Where mum would sit from dawn,
She waited here for many hours
When the little ones were born.

Dad made our two wee cots,
The little quilts were worn.
The lino on the floor was clean
Polished and a little torn.

Dad believed in miracles,
He knew the rain would come,
To feed our hungry thirsty land
Cracked by the boiling sun.

Mum stood so tall and proud
Yet her love was always near
Nurturing and devoted,
With a faith untouched by fear.

❧❦❧

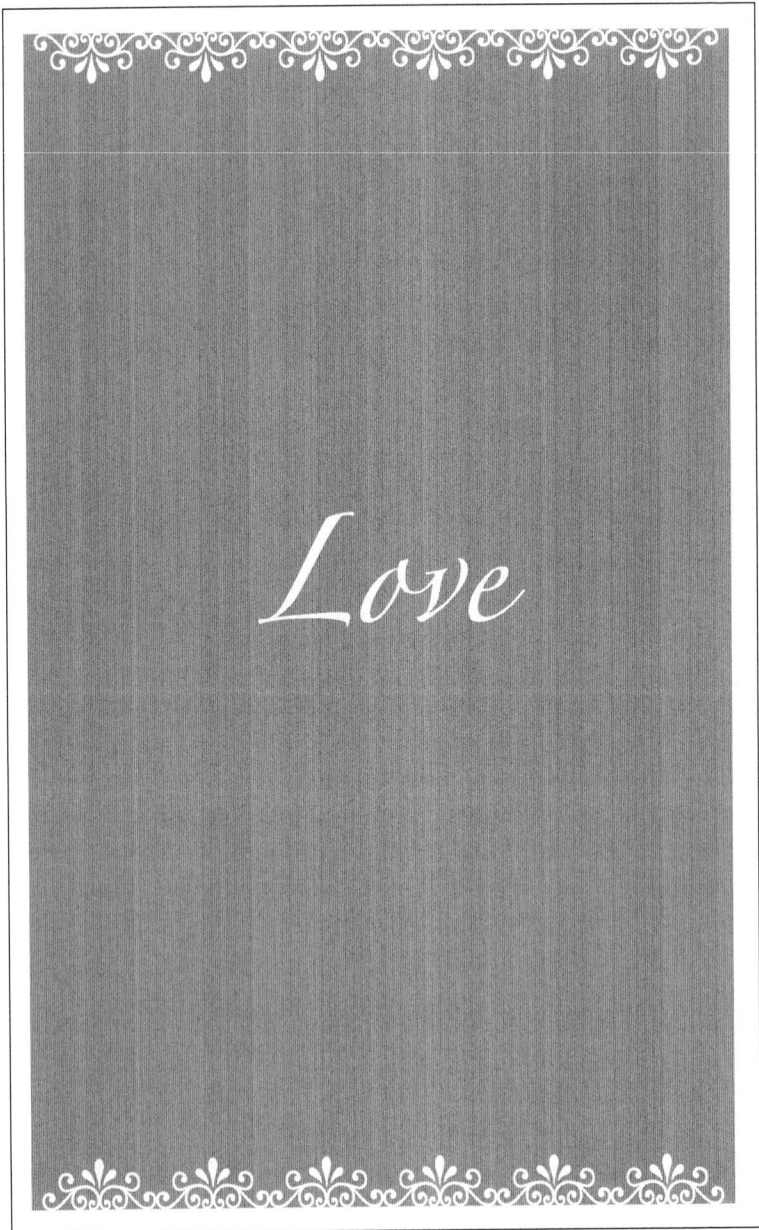

Love

Thanks for the Rose

Thanks for the rose you gave me,
With petals like velvet to touch,
Modest and frail in her beauty,
I love her oh so much.

But now she is quickly fading,
Her fragrance has passed away.
Dead on her stalk and drooping,
Her span has ended today.

᳇

*L*onging

I long for someone to love me,
For someone to stroke my hair,
I long for someone to kiss me,
I long for my bed to be shared.

I have no beauty to offer,
Nor am I blessed with grace so fair,
But a hidden heart within my breast
Beats passionately there.

Your picture lies under my pillow
Comforts me in my dreams,
Gives me strength to keep going,
However lonely it seems.

❧

Sunshine in Your Smile

There is sunshine in your smile dear,
A tremble in your eyes.
A light that shines forth from you,
Three years of love sublime.
Kneel before your altar,
Give thanks to Him alone,
For He has blessed you richly
With fame to shine your love.

❧

*S*ilent Retreat

It seems so long since you went away
And left me silently that day,
Not even a note did you leave behind,
Nor a rose petal of any kind.

I still long for the sound of your voice,
And the tread of your tiny feet,
But there is no you now, your choice
Was silent – silent retreat.

To the rest of the world I am happy they say,
Yet each night I cry since you went away,
My heart knows I shall never again see
The girl I loved who was all to me.

❧❧❧

*B*roken Dreams

There was a time when I believed
That you belonged to me,
Yet in a short duration
You broke all of my dreams.

You left me with our little child
When I was sick and sad,
You told me all those lies,
I know you're really bad.

When you were out of work
You never really tried
I didn't know you'd cheated
Until you were inside.

I gave you many chances,
You took me for a fool,
And now our life is ended,
You broke the Golden Rule.

෴

His Love for Her

You mean more than life itself to me,
I love you dearly, can't you see?
When I hold you in my arms,
You thrill me with your charms!

Those rainy nights when we met,
Holding hands that were so wet,
Your hungry lips pressed close to mine,
Your arms around me like a vine.

My love for you is life untold,
The pureness of your very soul,
Endows me with a love three-fold:
I love you, I love you, I love you!

❧❀❧

I Cannot Share

I shall not share the secret
Hidden in my broken heart,
Nor share the sorrow on my brow
That would dull the brightest lark.

Nothing left in me to give,
Though you offered me a part
Of your life, a hopeless task
Now to mend a broken heart.

Summer eases out the rain,
As most things come to life,
Yet my gloomy grief remains
On winters' shivering nights.

❧

Another Day

Tomorrow is your future
But to me just another day,
I sit for hours on this bench
To watch the children play.

With memories of past pleasures
My mind dwells in a way,
Of times we had together
On bright and sunny days.

One winter's night I strayed
Condemned me in her sight,
She would not forgive me ever
For that stolen night.

Her trust had been betrayed
The man she loved had sinned,
She jumped into the rapids
To end her life decayed.

It brought me to my senses
My heart was broken wide,
I'd lost my precious one
My soul felt dead inside.

❦

Forbidden Love

The vicar would never know
Within his sacred chapel,
The unrequited love she bore,
Burning inside her like a battle.
It revealed her inner beauty,
But he put first his Godly duty.
Lofty and rare were his ideals
She prayed all night and between meals
That one day she might at last find
Some sign that she was in his mind.
But while he dithered,
Her love withered
Never would he take a chance
There was no hope, not one glance.
And so with bitterness, and furrowed brow,
Her love and guilt ended now,
How painful were those sinful hours!

❧

Charms

Come to me my darling,
I need you in my arms,
I, who long to feel your beating heart,
Will never do you harm.

❧

Joanna

Dear Joanna, as you can see
I still have love just for thee,
And as the years go swiftly by,
I think of you as you lie
Dead upon your bed of ice.
And of the years you were so nice
To me, and all the others,
Who shared in the fame of Joanna?
If that's your real name!
There's no such thing as dust-to-dust,
For Joanna's beauty will never rust.
She lives still in memories untold,
For only Eros to behold.

❧

*F*ace of Noble, *Sweet Favour*

I gazed at you in your frame of gold
In Lord Digby's castle old,
I felt as though we'd met before,
That face of noble, sweet favour.

I go to sleep and in my dreams
I feel your lips and caresses stream,
A night of love with you my Lord,
With a face of noble, sweet favour.

You have passed on, I'm here to stay
Just for a while, then I may
See again as in days of yore,
That face of noble, sweet favour.

Yet I have no fear of death nor care,
I know you are waiting there,
Only time do I abhor
Until I see that face of noble, sweet favour.

❧

Memories

Suddenly I stood and stared;
Dared... to peep into that ill-lit room
In gloom… as I recall
The wooden chairs, and care-worn couch
All old and cold.
How could I forestall
The anguish in my racing heart
Bitter memories of it all.

❦

My Love

I prayed in vain to Heaven above
Having lost my one true love.
In grief and in pain,
He will always remain
My love: now up above.

❦

*B*ecause I Love You

You know my dear, why I shed tears,
The reason is, I love you.
Nothing else can give me joy
Because I need you.

You went away, no reason why,
My heart broke, I died inside.
I need you now, more and more,
Because I love you.

This void has left my heart in two,
I cannot sleep, thinking of you.
You are my life, my love,
Yet you fled like a startled dove.

We'll start afresh, give me a chance.
I love you but your final dance
Has left me weak, I need you
Because I love you.

౭ఌ౭ఌ

A Good Start

Love me and keep me
Never let us part,
Challenges we will face,
Right from the very start.

Let's make our life a song
With music in our hearts,
We'll always have each other
And never be apart.

With adoration and much faith
We'll never criticise or lie,
Or condemn or cheat
So our love will never die.

In trouble and in sickness
Let's face them all together,
We will overcome the challenges
Whatever is the weather.

This belief within our minds
Will give us a fighting chance,
For a life with deeper love
And everlasting romance.

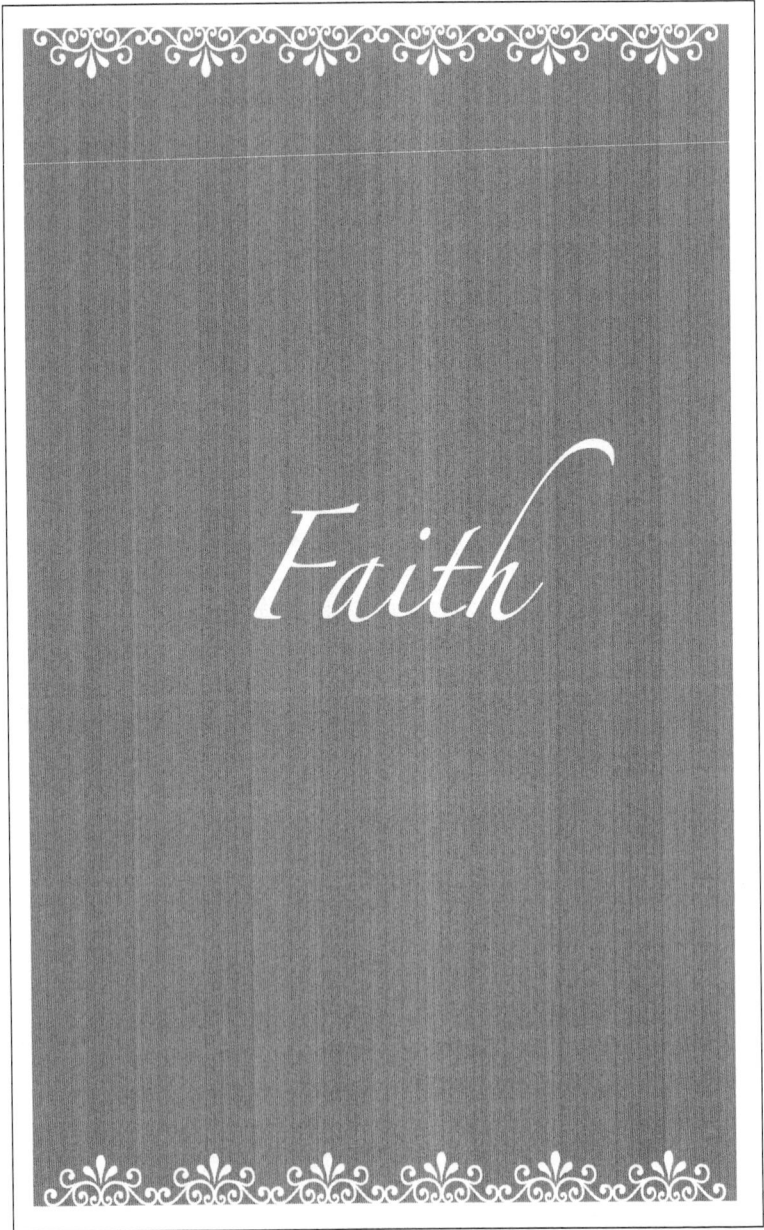

Faith

*F*aith

There was a child who silently prayed
At the foot of her trundle bed,
She loved the Lord Jesus, believing in Him,
He'd answer her prayers to be wed.

Patiently with no doubt in her mind,
She let the years roll by,
Until the day love captured her,
Oh! How her eyes did shine!

A few weeks of happiness
Then tragedy occurred.
Her husband killed when driving,
And to the grave transferred.

Why had God called him?
To a grave so damp and cold?
She looked towards the heavens
Her heart felt very old.

Would she lose faith in Jesus?
Condemn Him for taking him so soon.
Her beloved, gone just after the wedding
When love was all bliss and bloom?

But the love she had for the Saviour,
She proved as her life sped on,
"Test me, and test me!" she cried to Him,
"I'll prove that my faith is strong!"

When You are ready You will call me,
And into my grave I shall go,
I know I shall see my beloved
With You, on Your wide Golden Road.

❦

His Love

If you look forward to a life of fun,
Then keep in your heart faith in someone.
For He is above and can always be reached,
Never condemns, not even to preach.
He knows we are weak and forgives when we fail,
He holds out His hand, the one that was nailed.
Grasp it and hold it, and ne're let it go,
For great is His love as you'll come to know.

❦

$\mathcal{A}$ Hazard

The concept of man as a bearer of strain
Must testify to his faith.
But tension and conflict reign,
And man becomes a weakened waif.

We view life as a hazard
With never a thought for the Lord.
Creating conflict and tension
Shredding hearts like a sword.

In a sudden burst of sadness,
We see in a sun-lit sky
That life has passed us by.
Is there a reason why?

The sorrows and chaos of living
Are buried deep within our souls.
Seemingly empty and worthless,
Now too late to remould.

❧❧❧

A Motto

If you are sad and disheartened,
And struggling to be brave
Then let this be your motto,
From the cradle to the grave:

Cling to faith, hope and charity,
And live a worthy life,
Of simplicity and clarity
Free from any strife.

A powerful hand of any kind,
Will help you to transcend,
The agonies and miseries,
Teeming without end.

If your world is depressing,
Then cast your fears away.
And leave all your burdens,
For the one to whom you pray.

❧

A Man
with a Mission

A man with a mission: he hoped to be
A friend to all mankind,
Black, brown, or brindle, he didn't mind.
He set off to the country where the sun shined
Beneath the shield of burnished brass,
To him it had appeal.

Hushed air spread sunlight over the littoral,
The eerie moors whispered to gurgling streams,
For miracles to release them from their dreams.
A paradise of chattering birds, and grazing sheep
He prayed unheard in the wilderness
Then sank into a perfect sleep.

But when he awoke, rearing in the distant horizon,
Black chimney pots gloomed.
He drew closer to the city
Its nerves at breaking point.
He shuddered at the poverty, the waste and the blood
That ran through the gutters, in a filthy flood.

Hailed with sneers, no tear on their faces,
He'd never before seen one of these places.
His reaction was shock, his heart heavy too,
His mind in a whirl, what could he do?
He stood on the pavement in doubt and in dread,
Haunted by the ambivalence of the dead.

The stench in his nostrils, his belly felt weak,
Blood and muck was swamping his feet.
He was sick in the gutter, tortured in mind,
Just where to start, and where to find
This type of courage, to help mankind.

He prayed and begged to the Lord most kind
To give him strength and power of mind,
To purify and save this awful place,
With the help of these people he could revive
Not only their souls, but also their lives.

❦

Answered Prayer

As she watched her baby dying,
She called to the Lord in vain,
She never had cause to need Him,
Now she called Him, again and again.

He must have heard her pleading
As she sat in her room that day.
He knew her soul was bleeding
He would not turn her away.

As the Lord looked at her suffering,
He decided the baby to claim,
Then once more His name was called,
In anguish, grief and pain.

His mind was changed in a second,
He gave it the breath of life,
He knew He had gained another,
This miserable mother and wife.

For the look on her face was rapture
As she looked up to Heaven with joy,
She knew her prayers had been answered,
God had given her back her boy!

❦

Journey

Diversify your journey to the Land of Nod,
Fly further and feel closer then to God.
See many, many wonders,
Realise you are not alone.
Look into the heavens,
See God upon His throne.

The many beauteous visions,
Meant for human minds,
Let us try to emulate
And bc one of His kind.
Then many of His glories
Will be mirrored in your mind.

❦

Conflict, Doubt and Strife

Conflict, doubt and strife
Can devastate your life,
There's only one way,
That is to pray.

Conflict is sent for testing,
Trials we must embrace,
Conflict is sent as wrestling,
Challenges we must face.

Doubt is the red light,
Which comes on when we're low,
Only then through fear and grief,
We call the God we know.

Strife is a home of bleakness,
Unbalanced with turmoil,
Give and take a little,
Try not to over-boil.

So, with conflict, doubt and strife,
Banish them from your life,
Give them all away
And praise Jesus every day

❧❧❧

*S*aviour's Rescue

I sat upon the hill top
The wind was rushing by,
I pulled my rain coat up
To shield my watery eyes.

I had not sat for very long,
The earth began to move,
I let out a mighty scream,
Was this a dream?

I called to God
To save my life,
As He had done before,
A calmness overcame me
I felt God's presence near.
I knew He would appear
To overcome my fear.

❧

Jesus

Oh! Jesus I love you,
Each and every day!
Oh! Jesus I love you,
What more can I say?

You share my many burdens,
You rid me of my pain,
I love you dear Jesus,
I've so much to gain!

The path I have chosen
Leads me straight to you,
I love you dear Jesus,
What more may I do?

❧❀❧

Ringing for Jesus

Ringing the bell for Jesus
On a bright winter's morn,
Ringing the bell for Jesus,
Praise the day He was born!

Sleeping on His little bed,
Mary by His side,
Born to give His life for us,
He was crucified.

Not meant to live,
But meant to die
Remember Him,
By the bell's loud cry.

❧

God's Television

The world is the largest television
And viewed by God above,
He watches special programmes
Of youthful wars of blood.

He takes His time to turn the switch,
So engrossed is He in war,
He sees thousands dying there,
On the battle floor.

"This is what they wanted"
He said to His Son,
"If every man had stayed at home,
No war could have begun".

His Son said to His Father,
"Please change the TV station
To another human struggle,
In our beloved creation".

❧

A Question

Christ wept for people dying,
With not enough to eat,
Squatting on their backsides
In many of the streets.

And God cried out:
"Why don't they build dams
To catch the water drops?
Instead of sitting there for years,
They are a lazy lot!"

❦

*A*nd Live More Satisfied

Father and Son looked down in dismay
At this wicked generation,
"See how they are defiled!"
Said the Lord in agitation.

"I thought you'd gone down there,
All mankind to save,
Instead I see them sinning
More, and more each day".

"Murders, atrocities and lust,
They seem to love it all,
The Devil has been successful
In his plot to make them fall".

"I gave them a solid foundation
Told them to build upon the rock,
They haven't taken much notice,
This most ungrateful flock!"

"You go down there, Son
Show, and tell them what to do
I'm sure you'll be most welcome,
They will follow you!"

The Father called up Mary
From the human tomb:
"Take my Son back to earth
In your virgin womb".

Mary bore this baby
With an old man by her side
But little did Mary know,
That He'd be crucified.

꧁꧂

Abide with Him

The time was now ready
For the Son to tutor man,
But man was not willing
Or able to understand.

Alone He walked for many miles,
Till He met Peter and John,
Took them up the mountainside.
How His face shone!

Moses and Elias appeared
Just out of the blue
Then a presence filled the sky
The voice of God came through.

"This is my beloved Son
In whom I am well pleased".
And when the disciples heard this,
They fell down on their knees.

❧

Self-Infliction

In desperation these earthly mortals mourned their fate,
Bewitched by widespread destruction,
Their fate was sealed by Man himself.
Destitute of 'Moral Obligato', bereft of lesser laws
They added to the cesspit of which they stood in awe.

Devoid of wisdom and any grace,
These poor specimens of the human race,
Saw no running brooks, or flowered meadows,
All free, like the sun and the moon at night,
For them, the beauty of it all was out of sight.

❧

A Victim
of Bacchus

Oh God is there no respite in my tangled life
To ease the burden within my Soul?
Devoid of You, I behold a sinner's place,
With so little left to remould.

I mourn the days of my unrequited love
When Bacchus was my God, stifling me with
Ecstasies untold, I would unfold like a flag
Waving at each breath of wind upon my land,
With such an unsteady hand.

Enveloping rage and passion and seething,
With endless desires,
Have robbed me of reason:
For deep within my craving for just one more
To raise me to the regency of flight,
So Bacchus beheld my deplorable plight.

Frantic for the swirl of wine to suckle
As at my mother's breast, the burning liquid
Flowed again within my veins,
Where no noble thoughts could make their nest
Nor quench this fire of pain.

❧❀❧

Bereft of Passion

I am bereaved of passion,
Yet in my soul a lingering lust,
Nothing for friends to trust.
Burning sensations within my brain,
Begging for release from all this pain,
My span is short, my outlook grim,
Sinking into sex and sin.

My sensuous soul reared its head,
As I lay dying in my bed.
The ecstasies of all mankind,
I ache to leave behind.
My last thoughts are of birds and bees,
Brilliant flowers and chestnut trees.

I had forgotten to walk in the meadows,
Or to sing under the drooping willows.
Have I to bear this nailed cross
In trepidation while so lost?
Yes, it is too late, I can see
The Kingdom of Heaven is not for me.

ಌಜಜಌ

Token
Expressions

Grateful Son

A wish comes from my heart
With thanks for all you have done,
This is a greeting just for you
From an ever-grateful son.

❦

Thanks to Mum

When I was just a tiny tot
You took me in your arms,
To comfort me you held me tight
To shield me from all harm.
Throughout my days of childhood
You guided me with care,
I love you dearest mother
And need you always there.

❦

$\mathcal{T}$o Dear Dad
(From a Son at Christmas)

The things you taught me Dad
When I was just a boy,
Have remained with me forever
A guide to wondrous joys.

Your helping hand along the road,
Was like a gentle dove,
And all my life you stood by me
With everlasting love.

So have a happy Xmas
Be proud of what you've done,
I love you dearly Dad
From an ever-grateful son.

❧

Christmas Card Greeting

To wish you all at Christmas
Happiness on this day.
Enjoy this merry card,
And see what I have to say.

My thoughts are always with you,
Only love can show the way.
God gives us many blessings,
So thank Him on Christmas Day.

Friendship Christmas Card

Our friendship means so much to me,
A bond we'll never break.
As the years go by,
These Christmas ties
Bless you for Jesus' sake.

❦

*L*ove on
your Birthday

This message is personal,
Just to you from me,
Though we are miles apart,
Far across the seas,
I think of you everyday
Since you sailed away,
Come back to me my love,
Come back to me and stay.

WARNBOROUGH
PUBLISHING
18 Lower Bridge Street
Canterbury, Kent CT1 2LG
England, UK

Telephone: + 44 (0) 1227 762 107
Fax: + 44 (0) 1227 762 108

publishing@warnborough.ac.uk
www.warnborough.ac.uk

1976 -1996
Warnborough College
Boars Hill
Oxford

John Allen ~ The Rev. Canon Dr. Richard G. Martin SSC ~ Mrs. Diane Carter
Sir Christopher White, Bt. ~ Dr. Raoul Cerratti ~ Pastor Fred Smith ~ Rev. Dr.
William 'Bill' Chalker ~ The Rev. Michael Chantry ~ Mrs. Pam Hall ~ Dr. Philip
Cowburn ~ Mrs. Tommye Allen ~ Mr. Arthur A. Daitch ~ Ms. Eunice Davies ~
Rev. Dr. Karl Garrison ~ Mr. J.M. Gordon-Walker ~ Dr. Harry Gregson ~ Mr. Roger
Palmer-Evans ~ Dr. Thomas 'Tom' Imse ~ Dr. Richard Kirby ~ Ms. Sabine Liquard
~ Mr. Vic Markham ~ Mr. John McGeachie ~ Dr. Selma Al Gebali ~ Sir John Knill,
~ Mr. Ken Moore ~ Prof. Dan Mullarkey ~ Dr. James Oxley ~ Sr. Petrona
(AC) Schmitz ~ Dr. Judith Campbell ~ Dr. Joseph Bradford ~ Mr. John Michael
Taylor ~ Mrs. F. Rawlins ~ Mr. Norman Smith ~ Mr. William 'Bill' Walker ~ Mrs.
Esther Wright ~Dr. Graeme Tytler ~ Mrs. Lizbet Travers Cooke ~ Mr. Jay Allen ~
Mrs. Francis Welby-Fisher ~ Mr. Adrian J. Duffin ~ Prof. Eric Radford ~ Mr. Frank
Unger ~ Dr. R. Hollinrake ~ Dr. C. King ~ Mr. A. E. Keddie ~ Mr. S. Jones ~ Dr. H.
Jaafari ~ Dr. M. Garrett ~ Dr. J. D. Farquhar ~ Mrs. A.R.L. Broyles ~ Lord Pitt of
Hampstead ~ Dr. A. W. Adams ~ Mr. A. E. B. Turkson ~ Rev. Dr. Howard W. White,
~ Dr. King V. Cheek ~ Mr. W.G. Birch III ~ Mr. J. B. Carter ~ Dr. M. R. Golding ~
Mr. S.A. Jameson ~ Mr. D. E. Freedman ~ Mrs. J. Hall ~ Mr. P. Hanley ~ Mr. G. Coates
Mrs Barbara Frey ~ Dr. Roger Irle ~ Mr. G. W. Haley ~ Ms. P. C. Fenty ~ Mr. E.
Swrensen ~ Dr. T. McK. Lounsbury ~ Mr. C.F.P. Meaney ~ Mr. S. J.L. Potter ~ Mr.
Ian. C. Taylor ~ Mr. J. Wright ~ Mr. H. B. Towers ~ Mr. O. Brown ~ Dr. R.A. Younis
Mr. P.D. Chapman ~ Dr. A.R.I Johnston ~ Mr. R. M. Goodsir ~ Mr. J. S. Woolley
Dr. S.W. White ~ Mr. B.Y. Turton ~ Dr. J. Strawson ~ Mr. D. Sullivan ~ Dr. Alan T.
Rogerson ~ Prof. Raymond Maynard ~ Dr. A.R. Karlman ~ Dr. J.E. Oxley ~ Ms. Joan
Langley Smith ~ Ms. Peggy K. Cox ~ Dr. Gene Anderson ~ Major P. H. Middlemiss
Dr. Denis Paling ~ Dr. E. A. Little ~ Hon. George Vane-Tempest-Stewart ~ Mrs.
Betsy Mettee ~ Mr. John C. Carberry ~ Mr. A. C. Adcock ~ Dr. N. Dewey ~ Dr. M.
Henig ~ Dr. B. V. Street ~ Mrs. F. Russell ~ Ms. Sue Gardner ~ Ms. C. Coombs
Brigadier Douglas V. Henchley ~ Sir Anthony Weldon, Bt. ~ Dr. Geoffrey H.
Burne ~ Sister Gabrielle Sullivan SND ~ Mrs. A. Anderson ~ Dr. R.A.E. King ~
Prof. Margaret Frowe ~ Mrs. K. C. Blunden ~ Mrs. Kate Clipperton ~ Dr. Maxine
Marinaccio ~ Mrs. Phyllis Axelrod ~ Dr. R. C. Miall ~ Dr. S. Sadri ~ Dr. A.T. Taggart
Dr. John Mellon ~ Dr. P. R. Wheatley ~ Dr. Liz Christman-Rothlein ~ Mr. James
H. Gill ~ Dr. A. Gregory ~ Dr. Thomas J. N. Juko ~ Mr. Roland McCleary ~ Dr. S.
Mookerjee ~ Mr. Danny K. O. Ng ~ Dr. Emmanuel Santos ~ Rev. Donald M. Seltzer
Mr. Peter S. Thomas ~ Mr. Kurt Yeoh ~ Mr. R. E. Sainsbury ~ Mrs. Mary Jones
Dr. A. Liggins ~ Ms. T. Venables ~ Mr. M. Hugh-Jones ~ Dr. B. M. Hogemann ~
Dr. Anthony Marinaccio ~ Ms. Liz Brand ~ Mrs. Kathy Lubock ~ Dr. J. D. Green
Mr. Jerry Woodall ~ Dr. R. C. Finucane ~ Dr. A. L. Haldar ~ Dr. D. M. Holmes ~
Dr. K. D. Howlett ~ Dr. A. W. Levy ~ Dr. J. N. O'Sullivan ~ Mr. Don Mettee ~ Mrs.
Kathy ~ Mrs. M. Welby ~ Mr. Christopher Price ~ Mr. Earl Scott ~ Dr. Carmel T.
Thompson ~ Mrs. Sheila Hughes ~ Mr. Ted Cook ~Mrs. Gala Ladysheskaya ~ Mr.
William Pulfer ~ Dr. Nirmin Patel ~ Nana Osei Kojo ~ Mr. Peter Hughes ~ Mrs.
Carla Scott ~ Mr. Michael Walker ~ Mrs. C. Cruise ~ Mrs. Maude Rosenthal ~ Mr.
Jeff Nichols ~ Ms. Karen Dundass ~ Mrs. Susan Thornhill ~ Mr. Michael Kelly ~
Mrs. P. Turnbull ~ Mrs. Enid Tyler ~ Dr. P. Poobalan ~ Mr. Jason Cronshaw ~ Mrs.
Shirley Douglas ~ Mrs. Betty Thomas ~ Peter ~ Duke ~ Mr. Alan R. Mogg ~

Notes

WARNBOROUGH
PUBLISHING